Farmers Jok

The Ultimate Collection of Farming Jokes

Published by Glowworm Press
7 Nuffield Way
Abingdon OX14 1RL
By Chester Croker

Jokes for Farmers

These jokes for farmers will make you giggle Some are old, but most are new and you wouldn't have heard them before, and it is the largest collection of the very best farming jokes and puns around.

These jokes about funny farmers will prove that farmers have a good sense of humor, and hopefully you will soon be laughing out loud at these farming gags.

Disclaimer
All rights reserved. No part of this publication may be reproduced in any form or by any means without the written permission of the publisher. The information herein is offered for informational purposes only, and is universal as so. The presentation of the information is without contract or any type of guarantee assurance. Under no circumstances will any legal responsibility or blame be held against the author for any reparation, damages or monetary loss due to the information herein, either directly or indirectly.

FOREWORD

When I was asked to write a foreword to this book I was deeply touched.

That is until I was told that I was the last resort by the author, Chester Croker, and that everyone else he had approached had said they couldn't do it!

I have known Chester for a number of years and his ability to create funny jokes is absolutely amazing. He is quick witted and an expert at crafting clever puns and amusing gags and I feel he is the ideal man to put together a joke book about our crazy profession.

He will be glad you have bought this book, as he has an expensive lifestyle to maintain.

Enjoy!

Billy Goat

Table of Contents

Chapter 1: Introduction

Chapter 2: One Liner Farmer Jokes

Chapter 3: Question and Answer Farmer Jokes

Chapter 4: Short Farmer Jokes

Chapter 5: Longer Farmer Jokes

Chapter 6: Farmer Pick-Up Lines

Chapter 7: Bumper Stickers for Farmers

Chapter 1: Farmer Jokes

If you're looking for funny farming jokes you've certainly come to the right place.

In this book you will find corny farmer jokes and cheesy farmer jokes that will hopefully make you laugh. Some of them are old, but some of them are new, and we hope you enjoy our collection of the very best farming jokes and puns around.

We've got some great one-liners to start with, plenty of quick-fire questions and answers themed gags, some story led jokes and as a bonus some corny pick-up lines for young farmers.

This mixture of farming jokes will prove that farmers have a good sense of humor and they are guaranteed to get you laughing.

Chapter 2: One Liner Farmer Jokes

Being a farmer isn't for everyone, but hay, it's in my jeans.

Did you hear about the wooden tractor? It had wooden wheels, wooden engine, wooden transmission and wooden work.

As a farmer, I hear lots of jokes about sheep. I'd tell them to my dog but he'd herd them all.

Did you hear about the farmer who ploughed his field with a steamroller? He wanted to grow mashed potatoes.

Did you hear about the magic tractor?

It turned into a field.

I asked a farmer if it's easy to milk a cow. He said, "Sure. Any jerk can do it."

Why do farmers always have to put their gates in the muddiest part of the field?

Farming is really gardening for people with far too much land.

Money can't buy happiness, but it can buy cows which is pretty much the same thing.

I was really impressed by the scarecrow I saw the other day.

He was out standing in his field.

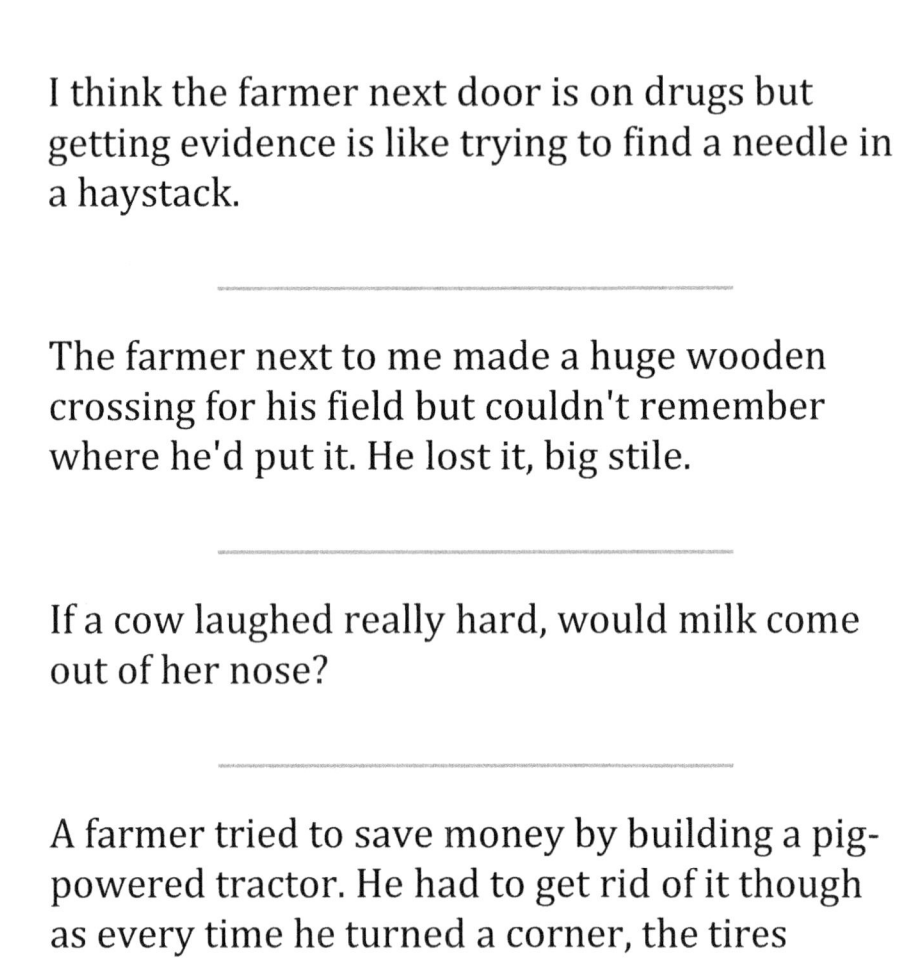

I think the farmer next door is on drugs but getting evidence is like trying to find a needle in a haystack.

The farmer next to me made a huge wooden crossing for his field but couldn't remember where he'd put it. He lost it, big stile.

If a cow laughed really hard, would milk come out of her nose?

A farmer tried to save money by building a pig-powered tractor. He had to get rid of it though as every time he turned a corner, the tires squealed.

A shepherd said, "I've got 47 sheep, can you round them up for me?

I said, "Sure, 50."

I got called pretty yesterday. Actually, the full sentence was "You're a pretty bad farmer." but I'm choosing to focus on the positive.

Farmers earn a meager celery, come home beet and just want to read the pepper, turn-ip the covers, en-dive into bed.

Did you hear about the new wonder bra they call "The Sheepdog"? It rounds them up and points them in the right direction.

A sign in a field near to me reads "The farmer allows walkers to cross this field for free, but the bull charges."

Did you hear about the cross-eyed farmer?

He couldn't see eye to eye with his livestock.

I couldn't get my tractor back home from work today. I drove into a magnetic field.

Did you hear about the young farmer who stole a calendar? He got twelve months.

A farmer's wife asked him to pass her lipstick last night but he passed her a glue stick instead by mistake. She still isn't talking to him.

An old farmer decided to buy the tax collector a new chair. The taxman will be in for a big shock when he plugs it in.

A farmer friend of mine gave me some great advice, saying I should put something away for a rainy day. I've gone for an umbrella.

Did you hear about the miracle of the blind farmer?

He picked up a hammer and saw.

Chapter 3: Q&A Farmer Jokes

Q: Why shouldn't you tell a secret on a farm?

A: *Because the potatoes have eyes and the corn has ears.*

Q: What farm animal keeps the best time?

A: *A watch dog.*

Q: What day do potatoes hate the most?

A: *Fry-day.*

Q: What did the farmer call his cow?

A: *Pat.*

Q: What do you get when you cross a robot and a tractor?

A: *A trans farmer.*

Q: What did the neurotic pig say to the farmer?

A: *You take me for grunted.*

Q: What do you call the best butter on the farm?

A: *A goat.*

Q: What did the farmer say when his fat pig wouldn't fit into the pen?

A: *There's more there than meets the sty.*

Q: What did the farmer say when he lost one of his cows?

A: *What a miss-steak.*

Q: Why did the farmer feed his pigs sugar and vinegar?

A: *He wanted sweet and sour pork.*

Q: Why did the lamb call the police?

A: *Because he'd been fleeced.*

Q: Why was the cucumber mad?

A: *Because it was in a pickle.*

Q: Why are farmers cruel?

A: *Because they pull corn by the ears.*

Q: How did the farmer find his lost cow?

A: *He tractor down.*

Q: What do you get when you cross a farmer and some trendy headphones?

A: *Beets by Dre.*

Q: Why did the farmer call his prize pig "Ink"?

A: *Because it was always running out of the pen.*

Q: What did the farmer give his sick horse?

A: *Cough stirrup.*

Q: What do you call an Arab dairy farmer?

A: *A milk sheik.*

Q: What do you call an arctic cow?

A: *An eski-moo.*

Q: What do you call a sleeping bull?

A: *A bull-dozer.*

Q: What is a scarecrow's favorite fruit?

A: *Straw-berries.*

Q: What is a shepherd's favorite vegetable?

A: *A border cauli.*

Q: What's the best part of farming?

A: *Getting down and dirty with my hoes.*

Q: What kind of pigs know karate?

A: *Pork chops.*

Q: What do farmers use to make crop circles?

A: *A Protractor.*

Q: What is a happy farmer's favorite candy?

A: *A Jolly Rancher.*

Q: What do you call a farmer with a sheep under each arm?

A: *A pimp.*

Q: What new crop did the farmer plant?

A: *Beets me.*

Q: What do you call a farmer who is happy every Monday?

A: *Retired.*

Q: What did the neurotic pig say to the farmer?

A: *You take me for grunted.*

Q: What grows under your nose?

A: *Tulips.*

Q: When is a farmer like a magician?

A: *When he turns his cow to pasture.*

Q: Why can't the bankrupt cowboy complain?

A: *He has got no beef.*

Q: Where do farmers send their kids to grow?

A: *Kinder-garden.*

Q: What happened when the farmer crossed a chili pepper, a shovel and a terrier?

A: *He got a hot-diggity-dog.*

Q: Who tells chicken jokes?

A: *Comedi-hens.*

Q: What is a farmer's favorite Bruce Springsteen song?

A: *Born in the USDA.*

Q: What did the baby corn say to mama corn?

A: *Where's popcorn?*

Q: How did the farmer tell his pig to take a bath?

A: *The farmer said, "Hog – wash".*

Q: What does a farmer talk about when he is milking cows?

A: *Udder nonsense.*

Q: Why do cows like being told jokes?

A: *Because they like being amoosed.*

Q: Why did the cow jump over the moon?

A: *Because the farmer had cold hands.*

Q: What do you get if you milk a forgetful cow?

A: *Milk of Amnesia.*

Q: What do you call a horse that lives next door?

A: *A neigh-bor.*

Q: What is a sheep's favorite game?

A: *Baa-dminton.*

Q: What type of horses only go out at night?

A: *Nightmares.*

Q: Why did the police arrest the turkey?

A: *They suspected it of fowl play.*

Q: Why was the baby strawberry crying?

A: *Its Ma and Pa were in a jam.*

Q: What is a horse's favorite sport?

A: *Stable tennis.*

Q: What did the farmer get when he crossed an owl with a goat?

A: *A 'Hootinanny'.*

Q: What do you call cattle with a sense of humor?

A: *Laughing stock.*

Q: What do you call a man who **used** to be interested in tractors?

A: *An ex-tractor fan.*

Q: What do you call a pig thief?

A: *A ham-burglar.*

Q: Why do cows wear bells?

A: *Because their horns don't work.*

Q: Where does a farmer get his medicine from?

A: *The farm-acist.*

Q: What do you get if you cross a sheep and a kangaroo?

A: *A woolly jumper.*

Q: Why did the farmer feed his cows money?

A: *Because he wanted rich milk.*

Q: What did the farmer say to his cows late at night?

A: *It's pasture bedtime.*

Q: Why does a milking stool only have three legs?

A: *The cow has the udder.*

Q: What do you say to a cow if it's in your way?

A: *Mooooooooooove.*

Q: Where do milkshakes come from?

A: *Nervous cows.*

Chapter 4: Short Farmer Jokes

I was driving past a farm the other day and there was a field with loads of sheep in it.

I said to myself, "Wow. Look at all those sheep crammed in there. There's too many to even zzzz..."

A farmer took his cross-eyed collie dog to the vet.

The vet picked the dog up to examine him and said, "Sorry, I'm going to have to put him down."

The farmer said, "Oh no. It's not that bad is it?"

The vet replied, "No, he's just very heavy."

At election time a coach load of politicians runs off the road and crashes into a field.

When the emergency services arrive, the coach is empty and there's no sign of the passengers.

The farmer is there with his tractor so they asked him what happened to all the politicians.

The farmer said, "I buried them."

They were taken aback, so they asked, "They were all dead then?"

The farmer said, "Well, some of them said they were alive but you can't believe anything a politician says, can you?"

An old farmer was walking down the path to the pond one day when he came across a frog. He reached down, picked the frog up, and started to put it in his pocket.

As he did so, the frog said, "Kiss me on the lips and I'll turn into a beautiful farmer's wife for you."

The old farmer carried on putting the frog in his pocket.

The frog said, "Didn't you hear what I said?"

The farmer looked at the frog and said, "Yes, but I'd rather have a talking frog."

Farmer:- "Have you seen the new film about the runaway tractor?"

Son:- "I haven't yet – I've only seen the trailer."

A sheep farmer and his wife were driving around Wales, looking for some good collie pups to bring back to England to raise, train and sell on.

At one point they entered a small town called Llanddewi Brefi and they just couldn't agree about how it was pronounced.

They decided to stop in the town for something to eat and a coffee.

As the waitress brought their orders to the table, the sheep farmer said to her, "My wife and I can't agree over how to pronounce the name of this place. Could you please tell us how it should be pronounced?"

The waitress put her tray down and said very slowly, "Buuuurrrger Kiiiing."

A farmer goes to the doctor with a hearing problem.

The doctor says, "Can you describe the symptoms to me?"

The farmer replies "Yes. Homer is a fat yellow lazy man and his wife Marge is skinny with big blue hair."

A guy was out in the country for a Sunday drive, took a corner too quickly and ran over a rooster.

Shaken, the man pulled over at the farmhouse and rang the doorbell.

When the farmer appeared, the man nervously said, "I think I killed your rooster, please allow me to replace him."

The farmer replied, "OK, You can go and join the chickens that are around the back."

A farmer was talking to two of his friends about their teenage daughters.

The first friend says "I was cleaning my daughter's room the other day and I found a pack of cigarettes. I didn't even know she smoked."

The second friend says, "That's nothing. I was cleaning my daughter's room the other day and I found a half full bottle of Vodka. I didn't even know she drank."

The farmer says, "That's nothing. I was cleaning my daughter's room the other day and I found a pack of condoms. I didn't even know she had a penis."

Did you hear about the farmer's boy who hated farm life?

He went to the big city and got a job as a shoeshine boy and so the farmer made hay while the son shone.

A young farmer and his girlfriend were out for a stroll in the pastures on his farm when they came across a cow and a calf rubbing noses.

"Boy," said the farmer, "that sure makes me want to do the same."

"Well, go ahead," said his girlfriend. "It's your cow."

A farmer asked his guest, "Did you sleep well last night?"

The guest responded, "No, the bed was soft and the air was fresh, but an old sow kept pushing at the door."

The farmer replied, "Never mind her. She always gets upset when we rent out her room."

An elderly farmer and his wife were leaning against the edge of their pig-pen when she recalled that the next day would be their golden wedding anniversary.

"Let's have a party, honey," she suggested. "Let's kill a pig to celebrate."

The farmer scratched his head and replied, "I don't see why a pig should take the blame for something that happened fifty years ago."

The farmer complained to his friend that his wife doesn't satisfy him anymore.

His buddy told him he needed to find another woman on the side, pretty sharpish.

When they met up a month or so later, the farmer told his friend "I took your advice. I managed to find a woman on the side, yet my wife still doesn't satisfy me!"

A kids adventure park was across the road from a dairy farm.

One day the kids saw a large bull and one of them asked the farmer, "Is that bull safe?"

"Safer than you are" was the farmer's answer.

A teacher asks a farmer's son a question in class "If there are twenty sheep in a field, and one gets out through a hole in the fence, how many sheep are left in the field?"

He replies "None, teacher."

She replies "There will still be nineteen sheep left in the field. Obviously you don't know arithmetic."

The young lad replies, "Sorry, teacher, but I do know arithmetic. Obviously you don't know sheep."

A farmer put up a pig-shaped weather vane, but instead of pointing with the wind, the pig vane keeps pointing toward the feed trough.

A lost hiker asked a farmer, "Will this pathway take me to the main road?"

The farmer replied, "No, you'll have to go by yourself."

Three ladies of the night are having a coffee break.

"I had an electrician last week," says the first. "The sparks were flying between us."

"I had a plumber last week," says the second. "He knew how to lay a pipe, that's for sure."

"I had a farmer last week," says the third. "First, it was too wet, then it was too dry, then it was too cold, then it was too hot and then he had to call someone in Brussels to get the money to pay me!"

A farmer's dog goes missing and the farmer is inconsolable.

His wife tells him, 'Why don't you put an ad in the local paper to get him back?'

The farmer does this, but after two weeks the dog is still missing.

'What did you write in the paper?' asked his wife.

The farmer replied, 'Here boy.'

I was in the pub with my sister the other night, when this really ugly looking guy came up to her and pinched her bum.

He then had the nerve to demand, "Give me your number, sexy."

My sister said to him, "Have you got a pen?"

He smiled and said, "Yes."

She replied, "Well you better get back to it, before the farmer notices that you're missing."

A farmer was milking his cow the old fashioned way, and he had a good rhythm going when a bug flew into the barn and started circling his head.

Suddenly, the bug flew into the cow's ear.

The farmer didn't think much about it, until the bug dropped into his milk bucket.

So, the bug had gone in one ear and out the udder.

On a rural road a policeman pulled a farmer over and said, "Sir, do you realize your wife fell out of the car several miles back?"

The farmer replied, "Thank Goodness that's all it is; I thought I had gone deaf."

A farmer's wife walked into the kitchen to find her husband stalking around with a fly swatter.

"What are you doing?" she asked.

"Hunting flies", he replied.

"Have you killed any yet?" she asked.

He responded, "Yep. three males and two females."

Intrigued, the farmer's wife asked, "How can you tell the sexes of the flies?"

He replied, "Well, three of them were on a beer can and two of them were on the phone."

On a drive in the country, a city slicker noticed a farmer lifting a pig up to an apple tree and holding the pig there as it ate one apple after another.

"Maybe I don't know what I'm talking about," said the city slicker, "but if you just shook the tree so the apples fell to the ground, wouldn't it save a lot of time?"

"Time?" said the farmer. "What does time matter to a pig?"

A salesman was trying to talk a farmer into buying a bicycle, but he wasn't getting very far.

"I'd rather spend my money on a cow," said the farmer.

The salesman replied, "But just think how silly you'd look riding around on a cow."

"Humph," retorted the farmer. "Not nearly as silly as I'd look trying to milk a bicycle."

A farmer was interviewing a young man for the job of assistant farmhand.

'You'll need to be fit,' said the farmer. 'Have you ever had any illnesses? Any accidents?'

'No, sir,' replied the young man proudly.

'But you're on crutches. You must have had an accident.' said the farmer.

'Oh, the crutches.' said the young man. 'A bull tossed me last week. But that wasn't an accident. He did it on purpose.'

A farm boy joined the army.

On his first leave of absence, his father asked him what he thought of Army life.

His son replied, "It's pretty good Pa. The food's not bad, the work's easy but best of all, they let us sleep real late in the morning."

Chapter 5: Longer Farmer Jokes

An old ranch owner farmed a small ranch in Montana. The Montana Wage and Hour Department claimed he was not paying proper wages to his workers and sent an agent out to investigate.

'I need a list of your employees and how much you pay them,' said the agent.

'Well,' replied the rancher, 'There's my ranch hand who's been with me for 3 years. I pay him $600 a week plus free room and board. The cook has been here for 18 months, and I pay her $500 a week plus free room and board. Then there's the half-wit who works about 18 hours every day and does about 90% of all the work around here. He makes about $10 per week, pays his own room and board and I buy him a bottle of bourbon every Saturday night.'

'That's the guy I want to talk to, the half-wit,' says the agent.

'Well, that would be me,' replied the old rancher.

A dairy farmer drove to the neighbouring farm and knocked at the door. A young boy opened the door.

'Is your Dad home?' the farmer asked.

'No, sir, he ain't,' the boy replied. 'He went into town.'

'Well, then,' inquired the farmer, 'is your Mom here?'

'No, sir, she ain't here neither. She went into town with Dad.'

'How about your brother? Is he here?'

'He went with Mom and Dad,' explained the young boy.

'Is there anything I can do fer ya?' the young lad asked politely. 'I know where all the tools are, if you want to borrow one. Or maybe I could take a message fer Pa.'

'Well, it's difficult,' answered the farmer, 'I really need to talk to your Father. It's about your brother getting my daughter pregnant.'

The young boy considered for a moment, 'You would have to talk to Pa about that, but if it helps you, I know that Pa charges $600 for the bull and $80 for the hog, but I don't know how much he charges for my brother.'

Three girls named Marie, Alexis and Brittney were driving through the country, when their car broke down so they walked to a local farmhouse to seek help.

However when Marie and Alexis get to the farm first, the farmer tells them they are trespassing and he raises a gun to their head and tells them to get a fruit or vegetable from the garden.

Marie grabs a turnip, and Alexis grabs a single grape. Just as they come back into the farmer's house, Brittney walks in. He tells Brittney to do the same as the other girls just did, and so Brittney walks into the garden.

While she's away, the farmer tells Marie and Alexis to shove whatever they have up their ass, and if they laugh he will shoot them. Marie laughs first, so the farmer shoots her.

Then Alexis laughs and she gets shot too. As they are floating out of their bodies, Alexis asks Marie why she died and Marie replied that the thought of Alexis sticking a turnip up her ass was just too funny.

Marie then asked Alexis why she laughed, and she replied, "I saw Brittney coming around the corner with a pineapple."

A small-town country farmer had a watermelon patch and upon inspection he discovered that some of the local kids have been helping themselves to his prized watermelons.

The farmer needed to discourage this profit-eating situation, so he put up a sign that read: "WARNING. ONE OF THESE WATERMELONS CONTAINS CYANIDE."

He smiled smugly as he watched the kids ran off the next night without eating any of his melons. The farmer returned to the watermelon patch a week later to discover that none of the watermelons had been eaten, but he found another sign that read: "NOW THERE ARE TWO."

Back in 1875, two sisters, one blonde and one brunette, inherit a family ranch.

Unfortunately, after just a few years, they are in financial trouble and in order to keep the bank from repossessing the ranch, they need to purchase a bull so that they can breed their own stock.

Upon leaving for another ranch to check on the possibility of buying a bull, the brunette tells her sister, "When I get there, if I decide to buy the bull, I'll contact you to drive out after me and haul it home."

The brunette arrives at the other ranch, inspects the bull, and decides she wants to buy it.

The rancher tells her that he will sell the bull for $499.

After paying him, she drives to the nearest town to send her sister a telegram to tell her the news.

She walks into the telegraph office, and says to the telegraph operator, "I want to send a telegram to my sister telling her that I've bought a bull for our ranch. I need her to hitch the trailer to our pickup truck and drive out here so we can haul it home."

The telegraph operator explains that it will cost 99 cents a word.

The problem is, after paying for the bull, the brunette only has $1 left.

She realizes that she'll only be able to send her sister one word.

After thinking for a few moments, she says, "I want you to send her the word comfortable."

The operator asks, "How is she ever going to know that you want her to hitch the trailer to your pickup truck and drive out here to haul that bull back to your ranch if you send her the word comfortable?"

The brunette explains, "My sister's blonde. The word's big. She'll read it real slow as 'com-for-da-bull.'"

A jogger is running down a country road and is startled when a horse yells at him, 'Come here buddy.'

The jogger is stunned but out of curiosity he asks the horse, 'Were you talking to me?'

The horse replies, 'Sure was, man I've got a problem. I won the Kentucky Derby a few years ago and this farmer bought me and now all I do is pull a plough and I'm sick of it. Why don't you run up to the house and offer him $5,000 to buy me. I'll make you some money because I can still run.'

The jogger thought to himself, 'Wow, a talking horse, that has to be worth a lot of money', so he jogs to the farmhouse where the farmer is sitting on the porch.

The jogger tells the farmer, 'I'll give you $5,000 for that old broken down nag you've got in the field.'

The farmer replies, 'Son you really can't believe anything that horse says. He's never even been to Kentucky.'

A Texan farmer goes to Australia for a vacation and while he's there he meets an Aussie farmer.

They get talking and the Aussie farmer shows off his big wheat field.

The Texan is unimpressed and says, "We have wheat fields that are at least twice as large as that."

They walk around the ranch a little more, and the Aussie shows off his herd of cattle.

The Texan is again unimpressed and says, "We have longhorns that are at least twice as large as your cows."

They carry on walking around the ranch when the Texan sees a group of kangaroos hopping through the field.

He asks the Aussie, "What are those?"

The Aussie replies, "Don't you have any grasshoppers in Texas?"

An old farmer had a wife who nagged him non-stop. From morning until night, she was always complaining and nagging about something.

The only time he got any relief was when he was out plowing with his old mule so he made sure he tried to plow as much as possible.

One day, he was out plowing when his wife brought him his lunch out to the field. He drove the mule into the shade, sat down on a tree stump, and began to eat his lunch.

His wife then began nagging him again. Nag, nag, nag, it just went on and on.

Suddenly, the mule lashed out with both back legs. He caught the woman in the back of the head killing her straight away.

At the funeral a few days later, the minister noticed something strange. Whenever a woman mourner went to talk to the old farmer, he'd listen for a while, then nod his head in agreement; but when a male mourner talked to him, he'd listen for a while, then shake his head.

This was so consistent, the minister decided to ask the old farmer about it.

So, after the funeral, he asked him why he always nodded his head and agreed with the women, but always shook his head and disagreed with all the men.

The old farmer said, "Well, the women would come up and say something about how nice my wife looked, or how pretty her dress was, so I'd nod my head in agreement."

"And what about the men?" the minister asked.

The farmer replied, "Well, they all wanted to know if the mule was for sale."

A sheep farmer is tending his flock when a city slicker rolls up in his BMW 4x4, hops out and asks, "If I tell you exactly how many sheep you have, can I take one?"

The farmer nods, so the city slicker opens his laptop, calls up some satellite photos, runs some algorithms, and announces, "You have 464 sheep."

Impressed, the farmer says, "You're right. Go ahead and take one." So the city slicker loads one of the animals into the backseat of the car.

"Now," says the farmer, "I'll bet all my sheep against your car that I can tell you what you do for a living."

A gaming sort, the city slicker says, "Sure, I'll take the bet."

"You're a consultant," says the farmer.

"Wow." says the consultant. "How did you know that?"

"Well," says the farmer, "you come from nowhere even though I never asked you to. You drive a flash car and wear a smart suit. You told me something I already knew; and you don't know anything about my business. Now give me back my sheep dog."

A young city couple is driving down a country lane on their way to visit some friends.

They come to a muddy patch in the road and don't stop in time, so the car becomes bogged down and stuck.

After a few minutes of trying to get the car out by themselves, they see a young farmer coming down the lane, driving some oxen in front of him.

The young farmer stops when he sees the couple in trouble and offers to use the oxen to pull the car out of the mud for $50.

The husband accepts and a few minutes later the car is free.

Afterwards, the farmer says to the husband, "You know, you're the tenth car I've helped out of the mud today."

The husband looks around at the fields and asks the farmer, "When do you have time to plow your land? Do you plow at night?"

The young farmer says, "Oh no. Night is when I put the water in the hole."

It was a bright sunny summer's day, and a farmer was busy tending his fields when a trucker rolled up and said, "Hey farmer, that's some mighty fine honeysuckle you have there. Mind if I grab myself some jars of honey?"

The farmer, thinking the trucker a fool, said, "Sure, you go right ahead."

An hour later the trucker came back with jars filled to the brim with honey.

The trucker left, leaving the farmer shocked.

The next day, the trucker rolled up again and said, "Hey farmer, that's some mighty fine milkweed you have there. Mind if I help myself to some milk?"

Certain that the trucker couldn't pull off the same feat twice, the farmer once again let him go ahead with a wave.

An hour later the trucker came back, jugs of milk splashing about in his arms.

The trucker drove away and the farmer was, again, left shocked.

The next day, the trucker rolled up again and said, "Hey farmer, that's some mighty fine pussywillow you got there. Mind if I help myself to some?"

The farmer was quick to reply, "Hold on - I'm coming with you this time!"

A farmer went to his local bank to borrow some money for a new bull. The loan was made and the banker came by a week later to see how the bull was doing, but the farmer complained that the bull just ate grass and wouldn't even look at a cow.

The banker suggested that he have a vet look at the bull, which the farmer agreed to.

Next week, the banker returned to see if the vet had helped.

The farmer looked very pleased and said, "The bull has serviced all of my cows. He broke through the fence, and bred all my neighbor's cows too. He's been breeding just about everything in sight. He's like a machine!"

The banker said, "What did the vet do to the bull?"

"He just gave him some pills," replied the farmer.

"What kind of pills?" asked the banker.

"I don't know," replied the farmer "but they kind of taste like peppermint."

A chicken farmer went to his local bar, sat down and ordered champagne.

A woman was sitting on the stool next to him. She turned to him and said, "How strange, I have just ordered a glass of champagne."

"What a coincidence", said the farmer.

He added, "It is a special day for me. I am celebrating."

The woman said, "It is a special day for me as well, as I am also celebrating."

"What a coincidence", said the farmer.

While they toasted each other, the farmer asked, "So, what are you celebrating?"

The woman replied, "My husband and I have been trying to have a child for many years, and today I found out that I was pregnant".

The farmer said, "What a coincidence. I'm a chicken farmer and for years all my hens were infertile, but now they are all set to lay fertilized eggs."

"This is amazing," said the woman. "What did you do for your chickens to become fertile?"

"I used a different rooster." the farmer said.

The woman grinned and said, "What a coincidence".

A farmer and his son are driving to the vet's office with their prize lamb.

They get to the office and the vet asks, "What seems to be the problem with fine animal?"

The farmer answers, "Well, he just seems to be acting strange around every time we go out to the barn to see him."

The little boy begins to sob, "Doctor, can you please help my poor sheep? We have been through so much together; I have raised him since he was only a few days old."

The vet reassures the boy, "Don't worry son, I have a machine in the back and if I put your sheep on it he will be able to tell me everything that has been going on with him."

The vet leaves the room with the sheep, and the boy sits quietly staring at the floor.

He then looks at his father and says, "I think that we should leave now. I know that sheep and I know as soon as it's just him and the vet back there he's going to tell the vet all kinds of lies about me."

A group of farmers, all aged 40, discussed where they should meet for a reunion lunch. They agreed they would meet at a place called The Dog House because the barmaids had big breasts and wore short-skirts.

Ten years later, at age 50, the farmers once again discussed where they should meet for lunch.

It was agreed that they would meet at The Dog House because the food and service was good and there was an excellent beer selection.

Ten years later, at age 60, the friends again discussed where they should meet for lunch.

It was agreed that they would meet at The Dog House because there were plenty of parking spaces, they could dine in peace and quiet, and it was good value for money.

Ten years later, at age 70, the friends discussed where they should meet for lunch.

It was agreed that they would meet at The Dog House because the restaurant was wheelchair accessible and had a toilet for the disabled.

Ten years later, at age 80, the farmers, now all retired, discussed where they should meet for lunch.

After some discussion it was finally agreed that they would meet at The Dog House because they had never been there before.

A breeder was taking a lorry load of sheep to a local show in southern England.

Just a few miles from the showground her lorry broke down, so she hailed a passing cattle lorry which fortunately was empty, and said to the driver she'd give him £100 if he'd take the sheep to the show.

The lorry driver agreed and loaded them up and went off, and the breeder started the long wait for breakdown service to turn up.

About two hours later she was amazed to see the cattle lorry come back and stop beside her, the sheep still all loaded up in the back.

She yelled "I gave you £100 to take the sheep to the show. What's going on?"

The driver shouted back, "I did but the tickets only cost £50. So I'm taking them to a cinema now."

Two brothers were sitting in a stuffy solicitor's office for the reading of their farmer father's last will and testament.

After a few preliminaries, including the disposal of a few small items to the cousins and some old friends of their father, the important part came: who would inherit the farm.

The crusty old solicitor took a deep breath, looked at the eldest brother and said, "Well, Timothy, the farm is all yours."

Timothy turned to his younger brother and complained, "See! I told you that you were his favorite son."

A farmer's son was returning from the market with a crate of chickens that his father had entrusted to him, when the crate fell out of his grasp and broke open.

Chickens scurried off in different directions, but the determined boy walked all over the area scooping up the wayward birds and returning them to the repaired crate.

Hoping he had found them all, the boy returned home, expecting to be told off by his father.

"Pa, the chickens got loose," the boy confessed, "but I managed to find all twelve of them."

"You did real good, son," the farmer beamed. "You left here with eight."

A farm boy accidentally overturned his tractor one day. The farmer who lived on the next farm heard the noise and yelled over to him, "Hey Joe, don't worry about it. Come and have something to eat with us. I'll help you get the tractor up later."

"That's mighty nice of you," Joe replied, "but I don't think Pa would like me to."

"Aw come on boy," the farmer insisted.

"Well okay," the boy finally agreed, and added, "but Pa won't like it."

After a hearty dinner, Joe thanked the neighbor for his hospitality and said, "I feel much better now, but I know Pa is going to be real upset."

"Don't be silly." the neighbor said with a smile. "By the way, where is he?"

Joe replied, "Under the tractor."

It was in the early hours of the morning and the ewe was heavily in labour but nothing was happening.

The farmer, fearing a complicated delivery, rang the emergency call out number for his vet only to find it was answered by a locum vet he had never spoken to before.

"This ewe is lambing and I think something's going wrong," shouted the farmer down the phone.

"Is this her first lamb?" asked the locum vet.

"No, you idiot!" screamed the reply. "This is the farmer!"

A farmer had worked hard all his life and in his retirement he is fulfilling his dream of having a new house built from scratch.

As he talks to the architect on how he wants the house built he says, 'See that tree there, don't cut it down because under that tree I made love for the first time.'

The architect says he understands the sentimental value of the tree and he will design the house so that the tree isn't harmed.

Then the farmer says, 'You see that other tree over there, I don't want it cut either, because her mother stood there and watched as we made love.'

The architect could hardly believe his ears, 'That's unusual, what did her mother say when you were making love to her daughter?'

The farmer replied,'Baaaaaa.'

A farmer was driving his tractor along the road towing a trailer load of fertilizer.

A little boy saw the farmer and asked him, 'What have you got in your trailer?'

'Manure,' the farmer replied.

'What are you going to do with it?' asked the boy.

'Put it on my strawberries,' answered the farmer.

The boy replied, 'You should come and eat with us instead - we put ice-cream on our strawberries.'

A Hindu priest, a rabbi and a lawyer were driving down the road, when their car broke down. They found a farmhouse nearby, but the farmer informed them that he had only one spare room, and that it had twin beds, so one of the three would need to sleep in the barn.

After much discussion, the Hindu volunteered to go to the barn. A few moments later, there was a knock on the bedroom door, and the Hindu priest explained that there was a cow in the barn, and as cows are sacred to him, he could not possibly sleep in the barn with a cow.

Annoyed, the rabbi volunteered to go to the barn. A few minutes later, there was a knock on the bedroom door. The rabbi explained that there was a pig in the barn and that he, being very orthodox, could not possibly spend the evening in the barn with the origin of pork.

Finally, the lawyer said that he would go to the barn. A few minutes later there was a knock on the bedroom door. It was the cow and the pig.

Two yokels were walking across some fields, when one of them noticed some cattle.

"What a lovely bunch of cows." he remarked.

"Not a bunch, herd," the other replied.

"Heard of what?" the first yokel said.

"Herd of cows," the other replied.

"Of course I've heard of cows." the first yokel said.

"No, a cow herd." the other replied, to which the first yokel said, "What do I care what a cow heard? I have no secrets to keep from a cow!"

Warning. Rude joke alert!

A stranger walks into a bar, and starts a conversation with an old guy next to him.

The old guy has obviously had a few and he says to the stranger, "You see that bench out there in the square? Built it myself, hand crafted each piece, and it's the best bench in town! But do they call me 'McStay the bench builder'? No they don't. You see that bridge over there? I built that, took me six months, through rain, sleet and fog, but do they call me 'McStay the bridge builder'? No they don't. You see that pier over there; I built that, best pier in the county! But do they call me 'McStay the pier builder'? No they don't."

The old guy looks around, and makes sure that nobody is listening, and leans to the stranger, and he says, "but you f*ck one sheep…"

An out-of-towner drove his car into a ditch in a desolated area. Luckily, a local farmer came to help with his big strong horse named Buddy.

He hitched Buddy up to the car and yelled, "Pull, Nellie, pull." Buddy didn't move.

Then the farmer hollered, "Pull, Buster, pull." Buddy didn't respond. Once more the farmer commanded, "Pull, Jennie, pull." Nothing happened.

Then the farmer nonchalantly said, "Pull, Buddy, pull." And the horse easily dragged the car out of the ditch.

The motorist was most appreciative and rather curious so he asked the farmer why he called his horse by the wrong name three times.

The farmer said, "Oh, Buddy is blind, and if he thought he was the only one pulling, he wouldn't even try."

A farmer in Wyoming had so many children that he ran out of names. So he started calling his kids after something around his farm.

At the first day of school and the teacher asked each child their name. When he got to one of the farmer's sons, the boy replied, 'Wagon Wheel.'

The teacher said, 'I need your real name boy, to which the lad replied, 'My real name is Wagon Wheel.'

The teacher, rather annoyed replied, 'Take yourself right down to the Principal's office this minute.'

The youngster pushed himself out of his chair, turned to his sister and said, 'C'mon, 'Chicken Feed', he ain't gonna believe that's your name, either.'

A guy was driving along a back country road when he passed a farmhouse, and before he could react, a cat ran out in front of him and then splat - he had flattened the cat.

Out of kindness and consideration, he stopped, turned around and drove back to the farmhouse to notify the occupants.

When the farmer's wife came to the door, he told her, "I am sorry, but I just ran over a cat in front of your house, and assumed that it must belong to you. I know this might be hard to hear, but I wanted to let you know instead of just driving away."

She said, "How do you know it was our cat? Could you describe him? What does he look like?"

The man promptly flopped down on the ground, and said, "He looks like this" as he gave his best shot at a dead cat impression.

"No", she replied. "I meant, what did he look like before you hit him?"

At that, the man got up, covered his eyes with both hands and screamed, "Aaarrrggghhh."

A city yuppie moved to the country and bought a piece of land. He went to the local feed and livestock store and talked to the proprietor about how he was going to take up chicken farming.

He then asked to buy 100 chicks.

"That's a lot of chicks," commented the proprietor.

"I mean business," the city slicker replied.

A week later the yuppie was back again and he said, "I need another 100 chicks."

"Boy, you must be serious about this chicken farming," the man told him.

"Yeah," the yuppie replied. "I just need to iron out a few problems."

"Problems?" asked the proprietor.

"Yeah," replied the yuppie, "I think I planted that last batch too close together."

Chapter 6: Farmer Pick-Up Lines

If I was a tractor and you were a plow, I would definitely hook up with you.

If you were a chicken, you'd be im-peck-able.

Would you like to switch the gears on my tractor?

Your father must've been a pumpkin because you look gourd-geous.

I'm not trying to impress you, but I do own a tractor.

Baby, why don't you come over here and ride my pony.

I'd like to grease you up like a pig and chase you round the barnyard.

The way you moo-ve attracts me like no other.

My name must be John Deere, because I'm totally a tractored to you.

Can we cuddle up? Because I'm Fresian.

I love your dairy air.

You have beautiful calves.

Do you live in a cornfield? Because I'm stalking you.

Your barn or mine?

Chapter 7: Bumper Stickers for Farmers

I'd rather be on a tractor.

Don't talk bad about a farmer with your mouth full.

Without farmers there'd be no food.

Save a tractor. Ride a farmer.

I'd rather be farming.

No farms, no farm girls.

That's it!

I hope this book gave you some much deserved laughs. I have written several other joke books and here are just a few sample jokes from my undertakers joke book:-

Q: If a snake and an undertaker got married, what would their towels say?
A: Hiss and hearse.

Q: Why does the undertaker drive his car slowly?
A: Because he's an undertaker not an overtaker!

Ever heard of the undertaker who accidentally dug up the wrong body? Well, he made a grave mistake.

Here are just a few gags from a book of mine unpretentiously titled 'The Punniest Joke Book Ever' which is available exclusively on Amazon:-

Trying to write with a broken pencil is pointless.

My wife has thrown me out because of my obsession with Arnold Schwarzenegger quotes. I told her, "I'll be back."

When I die, I would like the word 'humble' inscribed on the base of my statue.

About the Author

Chester Croker has written many joke books and he has twice been named Comedy Writer Of The Year by the International Jokers Guild. Chester is known to his friends as Chester the Jester and this book is a result of a challenge made to him by one of his best friends, a farmer, to write a joke book just for farmers! He can be followed on twitter @ChesterCroker if that's your thing.

If you see anything wrong, or you have a gag you would like to see included in the next version of this book, please visit the publishers at glowwormpress.com

If you did enjoy the book, please leave a review on Amazon so that other farmers can have a good laugh too.

Thanks in advance.

Printed in Great Britain
by Amazon

83012282R00058